User Training for Busy Programmers

Develop effective software training classes quickly and easily

William Rice

PUBLISHING
Birmingham - Mumbai

User Training for Busy Programmers
Develop effective software training classes quickly and easily

First edition: May 2005

Published by Packt Publishing Ltd.
32 Lincoln Road
Olton
Birmingham, B27 6PA, UK.

ISBN 1-904811-45-0

www.packtpub.com

Cover Design by www.visionwt.com

Credits

Author
William Rice

Commissioning Editor
David Barnes

Technical Editor
Nanda Padmanabhan

Layout
Nanda Padmanabhan

Indexer
Ashutosh Pande

Proofreader
Chris Smith

Cover Designer
Helen Wood

About the Author

William Rice develops software-training courses, user documentation, and knowledge management solutions. He lives and works in New York City. During his 15-year career he has worked with a variety of Fortune 500 clients. He specializes in training and knowledge solutions for software that supports business processes. This is his first book for Packt Publishing. He can be reached via his website at williamrice.com.

This first book is for you, Lisa. Thank you for encouraging me to stick with it.

Table of Contents

Preface

Training users is an essential part of software development but it's rarely a skill that comes naturally to developers. Even more rarely is it a skill that developers feel a personal drive to possess.

User Training for Busy Programmers focuses on results. Instead of teaching educational theory and leaving you to apply the theory for yourself, this book provides a framework for developing your courses. It's based on sound educational theory, but won't bother you with that. You will simply follow the guidance in the book, and end up with a well-designed training course that leaves your students equipped to use the software in their jobs.

No document can completely take the place of a qualified, experienced consultant. If you think that your training needs are beyond the scope of this document and your abilities, consider engaging the services of a professional trainer/course designer. On the other hand if you've found yourself with "software training" on your to-do list then this book is just right for you!

What This Book Covers

This book takes you step by step through the process of creating a software-training course. At each stage, the book focuses on deliverables that will feed into the next stage. Your course will take shape as you make the decisions and carry out the actions described in each chapter.

Chapter 1 discusses briefly the characteristics of good software training, and dispels some common myths and misconceptions about training. It then gives an overview of the processes we will follow throughout the book.

In *Chapters 2 – 7* we develop our course. Each chapter will guide you through a different aspect of developing your course. By the end of Chapter 7 you will have:

- Developed an audience analysis that tells you who needs to be trained
- Written the learning objectives, which consist mostly of tasks the students must master
- For each learning objective, developed one or more measurable criteria for success
- Developed a business scenario that will give your clients a realistic experience in the classroom
- For each learning objective, written an exercise that will teach that objective; one exercise may be used to teach several closely related objectives
- For each exercise, written an electronic slide show that includes many or all of the suggested slides; each slide show/exercise combination is now called a unit or chapter
- For each unit, developed a demo with detailed directions and speaking points for the instructor
- Written and packaged the Student Guide
- Written and packaged the Instructor Guide
- Packaged the slide show in a format that will play on the instructor's computer
- Tested the room setup
- Delivered the course to a small test group, or even an empty room; while doing so, you will have stepped through the exercises yourself

If all this seems daunting then prepare to be surprised. Developing successful training does require effort, but in this book I'll give you all the advice you need to make good decisions without stressful dilemmas.

Chapter 8 gives you some brief tips on course delivery, while *Chapter 9* draws the book to a close with a reminder of the key principle of software training: it's not about software, it's about helping users to get the job done—leaving them with easier and more productive working lives.

Conventions

In this book you will find a number of text styles that distinguish between different kinds of information. Here are some examples of these styles and an explanation of their meanings.

Code words in text are shown as follows: "Microsoft PowerPoint has a `Pack and Go` function that will package the slide show player with a slide show."

New terms and *important words* are introduced in an italic-type font. Words that you see on the screen—in menus or dialog boxes, for example—appear in the text as follows: Click the **Company Name** field.

> Tips, suggestions, or important notes appear in a box like this.

Reader Feedback

Feedback from our readers is always welcome. Let us know what you think about this book, what you liked, or may have disliked. Reader feedback is important for us to develop titles that you really get the most out of.

To send us general feedback, simply drop an e-mail to `feedback@packtpub.com`, making sure to mention the book title in the subject of your message.

If there is a book that you need and would like to see us publish, please send us a note in the **Suggest a title** form on `www.packtpub.com` or e-mail `suggest@packtpub.com`.

If there is a topic that you have expertise in and you are interested in either writing or contributing to a book, see our author guide on `www.packtpub.com/authors`.

Customer Support

Now that you are the proud owner of a Packt book, we have a number of things to help you to get the most from your purchase.

Errata

Although we have taken every care to ensure the accuracy of our contents, mistakes do happen. If you find a mistake in one of our books—maybe a mistake in text or code—we would be grateful if you would report this to us. By doing this you can save other readers from frustration, and also help to improve subsequent versions of this book.

If you find any errata, report them by visiting `http://www.packtpub.com/support`, selecting your book, clicking on the **Submit Errata** link, and entering the details of your errata. Once your errata have been verified, your submission will be accepted and the errata added to the list of existing errata. The existing errata can be viewed by selecting your title from `http://www.packtpub.com/support`.

Questions

You can contact us at `questions@packtpub.com` if you are having a problem with some aspect of the book, and we will do our best to address it.

1
Introduction

We strive to develop good training courses. But what is 'good training'? After 15 years in the software-training field, I've arrived at this working definition:

> *Good software training is when the students leave the class able to use the software to accomplish their business goals, and they have learned this in less time and with less disruption than if they had not attended.*

Good software training is not about learning how to use software. It's about learning how to get work done. And there is the difference between education and training: education is learning about, training is learning how.

A training class is worthwhile only if it saves the students time and trouble. Most adults are fast self-learners. They're also very good at integrating their learning with their work process. Your training course is worthwhile when it enables the students to learn and apply the material, in less time and with less effort, than if they had to teach themselves.

This book assumes that you need to design and write a software training class, and that you're not a professional trainer. It's also suitable for entry-level software trainers and course developers.

Consider this book to be a step-by-step coach, or job aid, for writing the software course you need in as little time as possible. It will not explain adult learning theory, or the instructional design system. It focuses on 'how-to' information instead of theory. The book assumes that you have time to learn theory later; right now, you need direction.

We began by defining 'good training'. We next examine the most common reasons software classes fail.

Misconceptions about Training

There are several misconceptions that prevent many software training classes from succeeding. If this book accomplishes nothing more than making you aware of these myths, you will still have benefited greatly.

Myth: Your Software Training Class should be about the Software

Your students did not come to your class to learn about the software. They came to learn how to accomplish specific business tasks. In the training profession, we call this approach as *task-oriented training*. We teach how to perform a business task, instead of how to use a menu option.

For example, a chapter called 'The Data Menu' pertains to learning *about* something, in this case, the Data Menu. 'How to Import Data', on the other hand, is learning *how* to do something, and reflects our task-oriented approach.

Myth: Your Students Want or Need to Know It All

The success of a training class is measured by the students' ability to be productive and not by the amount of material you covered. Saturating your students with information is not the most effective way to help them become productive. Your students need to leave the class with competency in all the basic tasks.

Research shows that one of the biggest challenges that workers face today is locating the information they need. Make the process of locating help and further instructions a part of your course. Refer your students to the online help, manuals, and other resources for refinements, shortcuts, and rarely performed tasks. During the class, focus on developing your students' competency in the core concepts and tasks.

Myth: In a Training Class, the Instructor Must Answer All of the Students' Questions

You don't need to tell your students the answers to all of their questions. You'll help them better by giving them the opportunity to discover some answers themselves. Adults are more engaged and learn more permanently when they discover some answers themselves. This approach is called *discovery learning*. You can give your students the freedom to explore in the class, while still keeping control of the class. For example, you can present a question during a lecture or demonstration, and then have the students perform an exercise designed to answer that question.

Myth: When Teaching Software, You Should Begin at the Beginning

This is almost never true and almost always done. Start with the background information, and you lose most adult learners within fifteen minutes. If you want to catch and hold your students' attention, start with something they can use. For example, begin the class with a demonstration of the process that they will learn, or by showing the documents that they will learn how to produce. Showing the end result of the class first is a good way to motivate your students.

Haven't we Solved these Problems with IDS?

In the training profession, we have a method for developing training courses called *Instructional Design System* or *IDS*. Some professionals believe that using IDS is almost a guarantee you'll develop good training. Others believe that the quality of a training course depends more upon the skill of the author than any system.

One of the major problems with IDS is that people have developed so many effective training courses without using it, and so many ineffective courses while using it, that it's hard for some trainers and managers to take it seriously. Others believe that if training is to be taken seriously as a profession, it must have a system for developing courses that can be applied in any situation.

This book takes the middle ground. We'll neither worship nor denigrate IDS. Instead, we present a plan for developing a course that uses the principles of IDS. But remember: this book is a job aid, not a course in learning theory. For more about IDS, consult a book devoted to the topic. You can also check out a few internet sites like (`http://www.ieee.org/organizations/eab/tutorials/refguide/ans01.htm`) for additional information regarding IDS. To develop a successful software course in as little time as possible, read on.

The Checklist

The checklist below is your map for creating the course. It is organized into short tasks. Each task is covered in a chapter of this book. If there are any supporting materials for that task, the section also points to those materials.

Copy the checklist, put it where you can see it, and start working your way through it.

Step 1: The Setup

The Setup involves making high-level decisions about your training course's goals and how to achieve them. Essential to this is obtaining the support of course sponsors.

[ ]   *Who needs to be trained*
       Arrive at a consensus about who needs to be trained and what kind of training they need.

[ ]   *Learning objectives*
       Develop specific, measurable objectives for the course.

[ ]   *Need for a training class*
       Determine if there is need that a training class can or should fulfill and that a training course is the right solution, or if mentoring, informal demos, or self-study would better meet the learners' needs.

[ ]   *Training scenario simulating business situation*
       Determine what scenario will give your students the most realistic experience in the classroom. Decide upon a training scenario that effectively simulates the real world in the class.

[ ]   *Learning objective exercises*
        For each learning objective, write a paragraph describing one
        or more exercises to practice that objective.

Set Criteria and Get Buy-In

[ ]   *Set the criteria for success*
        Decide how you will prove that the students have mastered
        each objective: by passing a written test, performing the
        process in front of an instructor, performing the process on
        the job, and so on.

[ ]   *Get buy-in from sponsors*
        Present the audience, outcomes, scenarios, exercises,
        and measurements of success to the stakeholders for
        their agreement.

Step 2: Develop In-class Exercises

Practical exercises are central to your course. Developing them first,
and then building the course around them, is the quickest and most
effective way to develop your course.

[ ]   *Prepare software for the exercises*
        Prepare the data files and application settings for class. Take
        a snapshot of the files and application so that you can
        duplicate the environment for your students.

[ ]   *Write the directions*
        Step through and write directions for each of the exercises.
        Save a snapshot of the training files after each exercise.

[ ]   *Revise the directions*
        Go through the directions and make sure that the following
        points are taken into account:

        o   Sentence structure: Put conditional phrases first

        o   Start each numbered step with an action

        o   State the result of each action

        o   Use the second person

- o Differentiate button pushes, menu items, and text that is displayed on screen

- o Separate nested menu items

Test and Revise Exercise Files

[ ]   *Return the training files and development workstation to its pre-class condition*
Return the training software environment to the condition it was in before you started writing the exercises. This includes the training application, data files, and any supporting applications and files.

[ ]   *Step through the exercise directions*
Step through the exercise from start to finish exactly as the students will in class.

Step 3: Develop Lectures

Next, we develop illustrated lectures to introduce each exercise. Gradually the course is taking shape...

[ ]   *Develop a slide show for each unit in the course*
Use the following list of slides as a guideline:

- o Unit Title

- o Purpose

- o When is this procedure performed?

- o Who performs this procedure?

- o What information is entered during this procedure?

- o What processing does the system perform on the data entered during this procedure?

- o What is the result of this procedure?

- o Special Fields

- o Demonstration

- o Exercise

- o Review

- o Questions?

Step 4: Develop the Demo

Most students will learn a lot by watching you perform actions. Develop demos that will give students the knowledge to perform your carefully chosen exercises.

[ ]   Identify the core functionality that the students must know to complete the exercise successfully.

[ ]   Write the demo directions and speaking points.

[ ]   Remove steps that use any menu items or functions that the students do not need to know.

[ ]   Consider adding optional functionality that you think will enhance the demo.

[ ]   Make a copy of the step-by-step directions for the exercise. Use this as the starting point for the demo.

[ ]   Change the data in the copy so that the demo uses different data from that in the exercise.

The result should be a two-column document for each unit, with step-by-step directions in one column and speaking notes in the other.

Step 5: Package the Course

Packaging the course by including handouts and notes gives it a more lasting value:

- A Student Guide means that students can refer back to course notes long after the course is over

- An Instructor Guide means that even other instructors and not just you, can deliver your course to students

The Student Guide

The following five components will remind your students of the course's key points, and where to get more help if they need it.

[ ]   *Write the Introduction*
         Cover the following points in the introduction:

- State the goals of the course
- Describe the intended audience
- List prerequisites
- State the duration and class size
- Include training group contact information

[ ] *Printouts of the slides*
Generate handouts, with several slides per page and space reserved for taking notes.

[ ] *Directions for in-class exercises*
Print out each exercise and place it after the appropriate slide show.

[ ] *Resources and contacts*
Include links to online help, where to obtain documentation for the software, and contact information for people who can assist the students.

The Instructor Guide

This consists of the same five parts as the Student Guide, and adds information to each of the parts. Start with a copy of the Student Guide and add the information below.

[ ] *Table of Contents*
In addition to a table of contents, generate a table of the units and their learning objectives.

[ ] *Introduction*
Add login information for any accounts used in the class. This includes the account for the instructor, the students, and any administrative accounts needed to set up the system.

[ ] *Printouts of the slides*
Print a copy of the slides and speaking notes for the Instructor Guide.

[ ] *Directions for the in-class exercises*
For each unit, place the directions for the demonstration between the slide show and the exercise.

[ ]   *Resources and contacts*

[ ]   *Slide-show files*
       Export the slide show in a format that will work on the
       classroom's instructor computer.

Step 6: Set Up and Test Run

Before delivering the course for real, it's important to test the material
and practice your delivery. Try to do as many of the tasks below as
possible. A full run-through may not be always possible, but if you
have the time, it will help.

Test the Room Setup

[ ]   Run the course software on the training room computers.

[ ]   Test the projector.

[ ]   Test Internet access.

[ ]   If the course requires Web access, test and ensure firewall
       and security settings do not interfere.

Practice Run

[ ]   Deliver the course to a small test group or an empty room.
       Step through the exercises and demos in the order they will
       be given.

Revise the Course

[ ]   Edit the course material based on feedback from your
       practice run.

Develop Follow-up Materials

[ ]   Develop the tools needed to measure the criteria for success.
       Get the sponsors' buy-in on the method or methods used.

Step 7: Deliver the Course

This last step is the practical implementation of all your above preparation. Make the most of your hard work, avoid embarrassing moments, and present a successful course by following the points mentioned below:

[ ]   Keep the tone consultative.

[ ]   Follow up unanswered questions.

[ ]   Avoid unexplored territory.

[ ]   Encourage students to watch and then do.

Summary

In this chapter we looked at the essential qualities of successful training courses, and dispelled some software training myths.

We then looked at a systematic process for creating successful training courses. We looked at a checklist covering the seven steps from setup to delivery.

We will begin to develop our course in our next chapter.

2

The Setup

This chapter gives you a list of goals for your training course and a high-level plan for reaching those goals. You will establish these goals and the plan with input from the intended students, their managers, and the sponsors of the course. Finally, you'll get the buy-in that you need from the sponsors.

Who Needs to be Trained?

"*Who needs to be trained?*" is the first question you must answer. Not "What do my students need to know?" or "When do they need to be trained by?"

In the training profession, we call discovering who needs the training and what they need to know an *audience analysis*. Many people who conduct this analysis assume that they have only one audience, with only one set of goals. Don't make this assumption. Your audience might include managers who need to know only what the software is capable of, users who need to know how to use it, and technical support people who need to know how to troubleshoot it.

Consider training people to use particular software for say, processing auto insurance claims. To accommodate different audiences, you might need a series of courses. Here are some possible audiences:

- Managers
- Users
- Sales
- System Administrators

- Technical and User Support

Here is a list of information you might include in the courses:

- *Business needs addressed by the software*:
  Example: "This application is used for the immediate processing of auto insurance claims."
  Especially relevant for managers, sales, and users.

- *Where the software fits into the business process*:
  Example: "This application is used for initial processing of the claim. Payment is processed in a different system."
  Especially relevant for managers.

- *Capabilities and limitations*:
  Example: "This application can process both single- and multi-jurisdiction claims. Do not use it to process claims for accidents that occurred outside the United States."
  Relevant for managers, sales, and users.

- *How to use the system*:
  Example: "To process claims with this system, start at the main menu..."
  Obviously relevant to end users, but technical support may also benefit.

- *Installation and uninstallation:*
  Relevant to system administrators and technical support.

- *Database structure and format*:
  Especially relevant to system administrators.

- *Interfaces to other systems*:
  Example: "This application draws customer information from the customer database. It passes approved claims to the payment system."
  Especially relevant for the technical support and system administrators.

- *Troubleshooting*:
  Especially relevant to technical support.

As you can see, covering the different types of information, and serving different audiences, may require multiple courses. You can probably think of other types of information that apply to the application for which you must train your audience.

Action

From below, copy the list of potential audiences and the types of information. Add your own items to the lists. Then, use these lists as a starting point for discussing the scope of the course(s) with the stakeholders and future students. Arrive at a consensus about the people who need to be trained and the kind of training they need.

Audience (Select One)

[ ]   Managers

[ ]   Sales

[ ]   Users

[ ]   System Administrators

[ ]   Technical Support

[ ]   User Support

Type of Information to Cover for this Audience (Select All that are Applicable)

[ ]   Business needs addressed by the software

[ ]   Where the software fits into the business process

[ ]   Capabilities and limitations

[ ]   How to use the system

[ ]   Installation and uninstallation

[ ]   Database structure and format

[ ]   Interfaces to other systems

[ ]   Troubleshooting

Write the Learning Objectives

For each class that you intend to develop, you must ask the question, *"What all do my students need to be able to do after this class?"*

You will probably have several answers to this question. That is, you will probably have several goals for each class. Each of these answers is a *learning objective*. Your answers to this question must be specific and stated in business terms. For instance, consider our auto insurance claim example. *"Use our new accident claim system"* is not an acceptable answer. Use which parts of the system? For doing what? Under what circumstances?

"Enter and edit claims using our claim system" is just specific enough to be reassuring. It's also ambiguous enough to allow the scope of the course to keep expanding until it's larger than you imagined. What kind of claims? When? Define 'edit'.

"Enter claims for in-state accidents, and edit the incident reports for in-state claims that are still pending" is a good starting point for developing a training class. It is specific about the business function that your students need to do, when they must do it, and the circumstances under which they must do it.

Each learning objective must specify:

- What business task the student will learn
- The circumstances under which the student will be performing the task
- The criteria for measuring whether the student has learned the task

Below is an example of a learning objective, written for a customer service system. The learning objective states one of the tasks the user must be able to perform. Notice that the objective reads as if it was written by a business manager, not by a programmer. Ideally, learning objectives should be determined by the business owners of the software. The following text explains how the objective meets the criteria for a good learning objective.

"When given a new customer contract, the student will be able to create the new customer and enter the contract details for that customer so that the data passes validation.

- o *Business task*: Create the new customer and enter the contract details for that customer

- o *Circumstances*: When given a new customer contract

- o *Criteria for success*: The data passes validation

..."

Here are two more examples of learning objectives. Notice that they both state the objective in terms of a job-oriented task:

"At the conclusion of this unit, the student will be able to enter a new purchase order into the system."

And:

"The students will demonstrate their proficiency in blending the end of one video clip with the beginning of another."

Checkpoint

At this point, you have developed an audience analysis, which lists the type of audiences to be trained and the kinds of information that each audience must learn.

Action

Discuss the learning objectives with the sponsors and future students. Develop specific, measurable objectives for the course. You may need to develop different learning objectives for each audience.

These objectives are the center of the course. Every word of every slide you write, and every step of every demonstration you develop, will support one of these objectives. Work with the sponsors to get them right before you proceed.

Is This a Need that a Training Class Can or Should Fulfill?

Not every knowledge gap can or should be filled by a formal training class. Knowledge gaps can also be filled by any one or combination of the following methods:

- Partnering the learner with an experienced mentor

- Arranging informal talks and demonstrations, given by experts within your company

- Supplying the learner with materials—and time—for self-learning

Notice that all of these alternatives require you to manage the learning process, instead of creating and teaching a class. At times, the best thing you can do for the learners is to create a situation where they can learn by themselves or from someone other than you. *This is not failing as a trainer. It is succeeding as a learning manager.*

Checkpoint

At this point, you have developed:

- *Audience analysis*: This lists the type of audiences to be trained and the kinds of information that each audience must learn.

- *Learning objectives for each audience*: These consist of the tasks the students must learn in your class. Each task is a learning objective.

Action

You may want to present the above alternatives to a formal course to the sponsors. Perhaps they are asking for a formal training class only because they have never thought of alternatives. Consider your situation and act accordingly.

What Scenario will give your Clients the Most Realistic Experience in the Classroom?

In this section, we discuss how to decide upon a business scenario that you will use to teach the tasks. Look at the process your students must master and ask, "*How can I simulate the real world in class?*"

Your goal is to develop a scenario for the training exercises that will take your clients through the entire process that they must learn. An effective training scenario answers the question, "*What does this job look like when it's done right?*". It involves the following two steps.

Define the Process

Organize your tasks, or learning objectives into a logical sequence if you haven't already done so.

You might want to work with a subject matter expert to determine the sequence in which the students will complete the tasks on the job. Alternatively, the circumstances might mean that you yourself are the expert. For the time being, we will assume that you, the course developer, and the subject matter expert are different people.

After the tasks have been arranged in a sequence, determine if there are any transitional tasks that must be completed in between the ones you have. For example, suppose your first and second learning objectives are "*Create a new claim*" and "*Pass the claim on to the examiner*". When the students are on the job, will they need to complete any other tasks between these two? Will they need to validate the claim before passing it on? Or notify anyone else of the claim? Work with the expert to fill in these blanks. Focus on identifying the tasks. Do not yet write detailed step-by-step directions for them.

The result should be a sequence of tasks that the student completes on the job. These tasks describe the process that you must teach your students.

One Process or Several?

If the tasks are always, or almost always, done in the same order, then designing your teaching scenario is much easier. If the process branches, your teaching scenario will probably need to be more complex. In the auto insurance claim example used above, you would need to determine whether claims are always entered the same way, or whether the process changes based upon the type of claim. That is, are you teaching one process or several?

The tasks themselves might also change. To use our claim system example again, the task of validating a claim might be different for claims made in different cities.

At this point, you must decide if you are teaching one process or many. If you are teaching one process, your job is much easier.

If you need to teach several processes, then you must decide whether each process needs to be taught in a different class. If the different processes will be taught to different audiences, then consider developing a different class for each process/audience combination. Customize each class to its audience.

If you need to teach several processes to the same group, consider organizing the course to teach the core, or simplest, process first. Then, revisit the process and teach the variations at the end of class.

Checkpoint

At this point, you have developed:

- An audience analysis, which lists the type of audiences to be trained and the kinds of information that each audience must learn

- The learning objectives for each audience, which consist of the tasks the students must learn in your class. Each task is a learning objective

- A consensus among the sponsors that a structured training class really is the best way for the students to learn these tasks

Action

After completing this section, you should have two results. The first is a decision. Are you teaching:

- One process to one audience?
- Different processes to different audiences?
- Several processes to one audience?

The second result should be a sequence of tasks that describe each of the process(es) the students complete on the job. If you haven't decided to teach multiple processes, then this is unchanged from the previous section.

Develop a Training Scenario

Now it is time to develop a training scenario that you can use to teach the process.

What is a Training Scenario?

In software training, your goal is to develop competence in a specific process or set of tasks. The exercises that your clients practice these skills on are what build their competence. The slides, handouts, and lectures support the exercises. For each class you need to design a training scenario that is appropriate for the process and tasks to be taught in that class.

This scenario should simulate a business situation that the students will face. In our auto insurance claim example, the scenario could involve processing several different types of claims. When designing this scenario, we would describe each type of claim and list any special features of the application that the claim uses.

Your scenario design will read almost like a narrative of a day in the life of your student. Remember that the scenario is a summary, or description, of a business situation. It is not step-by-step directions for using the application.

The following example is a part of a training scenario. In this scenario, the course teaches users how to process insurance claims. Notice that the scenario covers variations of one task: processing a claim.

Notice also that the scenario addresses the workflow for these claims. It states what tasks the user will do, in what order, without telling us how:

> "The student will process a variety of in-state and out-of-state claims, involving both at-fault and no-fault claims. Some claims will require investigation. The student will identify these claims and, using the software's process control features, hand them off to the appropriate parties..."

Don't confuse the overall scenario with an individual exercise. The scenario is the setting for all of the exercises. Each exercise teaches one of the tasks, or learning objectives.

The following example describes the usage of a new online requisition system. Notice that this scenario tells us where the requisition system fits into the larger business process of purchasing supplies for a given company. The scenario takes the users through the entire process of using the software, from entering a requisition to receiving the requisitioned items:

> "The student will enter and track several purchase orders through the system. Using their own user ID, a fictional vendor, and a fictional training fund, the user will enter a purchase order for a large capital purchase that requires approval at both Departmental and Finance levels.
>
> The instructor will provide the approvals in class. After approval is granted, the student will be instructed to log into their account and check the status of the purchase order. They will then use the online fax capability to order the item from the fictional vendor. The instructor will then change the status of the order to Delivered, and instruct the student to check the status again.
>
> The goal of this scenario is to simulate the entire purchase order process, from placing the order through approval to final delivery."

During this scenario, the instructor plays the role of other people involved in the requisition process. On the job, the requisitions entered by the users require approval from the *Department* and from *Finance*. To simulate this approval, the instructor will play those roles.

Notice also that the instructor will "change the status of the order to `Delivered`". The software must be set up so that the instructor can give these approvals and change the status during the class. The scenario designer must consider how many requisitions the students will create in the class, and how long it will take the instructor to simulate the approval and delivery of these requisitions.

The following example is another training scenario:

"The training scenario used in the class will simulate the process of retrieving sales data from a database. The students will search for regions whose sales exceed or fail to meet projections by a given percentage, for a given time period. They will then drill down into these regions and locate the individual locations that are responsible for the variances. Finally, they will extract the relevant regional and location sales data to spreadsheet files and present it in graphical form."

A Special Case: Software Toolkits

If you're not teaching a software toolkit, you can safely skip this section. Software toolkits present a special training challenge. When teaching a toolkit, you're not teaching a predictable process. You're teaching a set of tools and techniques that can be used in many, unpredictable ways.

An *Application Programming Interface (API)* is one example of toolkit training. A programming language is another. In these courses, each function or group of functions would comprise one chapter. The question is how do we design the scenario for our in-class practice so that it flows logically, and gives the students experience with the many possible ways of using the functions?

End-user training is like teaching someone how to build a wooden box. You might need to teach how to put the hinges in different places or how to attach different clasps, but the basic process is very predictable.

Software toolkit training is like teaching someone how to use the woodworking tools in a shop. It's difficult to predict how your students might want to use and combine those tools. How do you ensure that

25

they leave knowing how to build whatever they desire, whether it is a box or a table?

This unpredictability makes scenarios for software toolkit training very difficult to develop. You have many options for developing scenarios for a toolkit course. As usual, the options that are best for your students require the most work from you.

Developing a toolkit course around the single most probable usage of each item you are teaching is the easiest option. Design each in-class exercise to demonstrate the most probable usage of the function or group of functions. Don't make the output of one exercise become the input for another, or make all the exercises part of a common scenario. Instead, design each exercise to stand alone.

Leave time to discuss more exotic usages in the class. After each exercise, encourage the students to ask about how the function(s) can be applied to their situations. This usually gives satisfactory results...*if* the course designer leaves enough time in the schedule for discussion, and *if* the instructor prepares for questions by learning the students' situations before the class.

When using this option, student satisfaction can be greatly increased if you give them a choice of exercises to work through at the end of the class. Each exercise can simulate the situation of one type of client.

Here is how the flow of the class would look:

1. You lecture and demonstrate one function or group of functions.

2. The students complete an exercise for that function. The exercise demonstrates the most probable or popular usage of that function. The exercise also stands alone: it does not depend upon a previous exercise for its input and its output is not used in any other exercises.

3. After all functions have been taught and practiced, the students choose from a variety of exercises that use multiple functions. Each exercise focuses on a unique business situation. You'll need to develop several kinds of end-of-class scenarios.

The Scenario

Why are we talking about the scenario before we've even written the course outline? Because the practice scenario is the outline.

Checkpoint

At this point, you should:

- Know what tasks the students must learn in your class

- Know that a structured training class or classes really is the best way for the students to learn these tasks

- Have listed learning objectives, and obtained the stakeholder's agreement upon them

Action

Now it is time to write a training scenario that simulates the business situation that the students will practice in class.

Write an Exercise Description for Each Learning Objective

The scenario represents the overall process the students must learn. That process consists of a series of tasks, which you have already defined. Each task or learning objective needs a practice exercise. An in-class exercise is to your software class what a word problem is to a math class.

After writing the scenario, you will get out your list of objectives, sit down with your subject expert, and write a few paragraphs describing the exercise for each task.

The following example is a part of a training exercise description. During this exercise, the user enters information about an automobile accident. The entire exercise can be accomplished on one screen. Notice that the exercise description does not consist of step-by-step directions. For now, it's just a word problem. We'll write the detailed directions later.

"An accident claim involving two drivers who both have Acme insurance is filed by Driver 1. Driver 2 is the party at fault. Property damage is estimated at $2,000. There were no injuries..."

During most exercises, you will want the student to interact with a single screen. If you write an exercise description and see that the student would need to navigate to an entirely different screen to complete the exercise, consider breaking it into smaller exercises.

Examples of Learning Objectives and Exercise Descriptions

Notice that each of the following exercise descriptions states the input the student will be given, the processing the student should perform, and how the output will be evaluated.

Example 1

Based upon the information available, the student will create a purchase order. The instructor will review each purchase order, and approve it in class, to enable the student to see the results of the approval process.

Objective

At the conclusion of this unit, the student will be able to enter a new purchase order into the system.

Exercise Description

The student will be supplied with the following information:

- Name of the vendor from whom the item is being ordered
- Name of the person within the company for whom the item is being ordered
- Item description, catalog number, price, and quantity
- Fund to which the expense applies

The fund that the student uses for this exercise should be a fictitious fund, to avoid using real funds in training.

Example 2

The student will blend the last two seconds of one supplied video clip with the first two seconds of another. The student will save the resulting clip for the instructor's review.

Objective

The student will demonstrate proficiency in blending the end of one video clip with the beginning of another.

Exercise Description

The student will be supplied with two video clips, whose filenames will be clip1.mpg and clip2.mpg. The student will be instructed to blend the last two seconds of clip1 into the first two seconds of clip2, and save the resultant output as blended_[studentname].mpg. The student should then copy the clip to the f:/classfiles folder for review by the instructor.

Checkpoint

At this point, you should:

- Know what tasks the students must learn in your class

- Know that a structured training class or classes really is the best way for the students to learn these tasks

- Have listed learning objectives, and obtained the stakeholder's agreement upon them

- Have described a training scenario that simulates the business situation that the students will practice in class

Action

Now it is time to write a paragraph describing one or more exercises to practice each learning objective

Set the Criteria for Success

You have stated the tasks or learning objectives for your course. You have designed a scenario for the course. For each task, you have a brief description of an exercise that will be used to teach the task. It is time to work with the sponsors to set criteria for determining whether your course has succeeded. That is, it is time to answer the question: "*How will I prove that the students have mastered each objective?*"

This is called the course's *criteria for success*. Some examples of criteria for success are when the students:

- Pass a written test
- Perform the process taught in front of an instructor
- Perform the process taught while on the job

Each of these is a 'measurable result'. In each case, you can point to objective evidence that the course met its agreed-upon criteria for success. In all cases, you must work with the sponsors to determine those criteria.

We cannot discuss setting the criteria for success without also discussing how to measure those criteria.

The written test and performing the process in front of an instructor are easy criteria to measure. If this is done at the end of class, before the students leave, you are almost guaranteed that every student will be properly evaluated. However, the traditional end-of-class test does not measure the long-term effectiveness of the training.

The most difficult to measure and the most meaningful criterion for success is the students' on-the-job performance. It is also more difficult to arrange this kind of evaluation. Make sure that you can overcome the logistic difficulties before agreeing to make this part of the course's criteria for success.

On-the-job effectiveness can be measured by asking the students' managers to evaluate the students' performance of the tasks taught in the class. Again, before agreeing to make on-the-job effectiveness a criterion for success, make sure you have the tools and opportunity to measure it.

Action: Write Criteria for Success

Retrieve your list of learning objectives. You have at least one exercise paired with each learning objective. Now you need to write at least one measurable criterion for success for each objective.

For example, consider the following objective:

> "When given a new customer contract, the student will be able to create the new customer and enter the contract details for that customer so that the data passes validation."

You could establish either or both of the following criteria for success for the above objective:

> "Given a list of steps for creating a new customer, the student will place the steps in the correct order."

> "Given contract details in the workbook or handout, the student will create a new contract in the class without help from the instructor."

For each learning objective, write one or more of these criteria.

Checkpoint

At this point, you have developed:

- An audience analysis that tells you who needs to be trained

- The learning objectives, which consist mostly of tasks the students must master

- A business scenario that will give your clients a realistic experience in the classroom

- A short description of an exercise for each learning objective that will teach that objective

- Measurable criteria for success for each learning objective,

After accomplishing all of these preliminaries, you will be tempted to forge ahead with developing the training materials. However, you have one more thing to do before you can start writing material.

Get Buy-in from Sponsors

The stakeholders—the managers who are sponsoring this course—must have a chance to agree to the audience, outcomes, scenarios, exercises, and measurements of success. You should be able to present these five items to management in a short report.

The most important reason for getting buy-in from managerial-level stakeholders can be summed up in one word: *authority*. To compile your training material, you will need the cooperation of subject matter experts. To schedule and physically set up for the course, you will need cooperation from administrators. And to fill the course, you will need cooperation from the students and their managers. As you can see, taking a training course from conception to evaluation requires a lot of cooperation and negotiation. It's much easier getting cooperation when upper-level sponsors have explicitly expressed support for the items in your plan.

Summary

In this chapter we saw how to lay the foundation for a successful software course. We learned how to identify the needs that our course must fulfill. We learned to develop training scenarios that will be a strong simulation of real business use and develop these scenarios into specific exercises.

Next, we saw how to set criteria for assessing a student's success at each of the objectives. Finally, we explored the importance of getting buy-in from the course sponsors.

In the next chapter we will look at how to develop the exercises into fully prepared tasks for your students.

3

Develop In-class Exercises

At this point, most books on training would instruct you to develop a detailed course outline. After you have an outline that is two or three levels deep, the course almost writes itself. This book will make no such recommendation, for two reasons.

First, because the organization and content of the course are based upon the exercises, it makes sense to start writing with the exercises.

Second, in today's fast-paced, budget-conscious environment, very few course writers have time to lovingly craft a detailed course outline before producing actual course material.

Forget what your grade-school writing teacher told you about beginning a writing project with a detailed outline, and starting with the beginning. The exercises are central to the course, so that is where we will begin: in the middle, with the exercises.

Prepare Software for the Exercises

Congratulations! You have a detailed plan for the course, and the buy-in on that plan from those who are depending upon you. At this point, you are almost unstoppable.

Your next task is gathering the data files and applications needed for the exercises. In our auto insurance processing example, you would need the following:

- The claims-processing application

- The correct configuration for the application with proper processing rules for whichever type of claims and locations will be used in the exercises

- Customers added to the application's database

- A user ID for the application, with the same access rights that your students will have

You need to compile a similar list of software requirements for your class.

After compiling your list of requirements for the training environment, install the software on the computer that you will use to develop the training exercises. Then, before you start developing the exercises, take a snapshot of the training system. That is, back up or copy the application's data and settings files.

This system snapshot of your starting point is important because of the following reasons:

- If you find yourself going down the wrong path while developing the exercises, you can easily restore your system to its original starting point and start over.

- If development of the exercises goes well, you can use the snapshot as the starting point for the training computers.

Checkpoint

At this point, you have developed:

- An audience analysis that tells you who needs to be trained

- The learning objectives, which consist mostly of tasks the students must master

- A business scenario that will give your clients a realistic experience in the classroom

- A short description of an exercise for each learning objective that will teach that objective

- Measurable criteria for success for each learning objective

- Consensus among the course's sponsors for all of the above

Action

Prepare the data files and application settings for the class. Take a snapshot of the files and application so that you can duplicate the environment for your students.

Write the Directions

At this point, you will write directions for each of the exercises. This requires you to use the same software that your clients will use in class, log into it with the same privileges, and start with the same data files. You then step through the detailed description for each exercise, in order. You will write each step as you complete it.

Save a Version of the Data after Each Exercise

If you are developing end-user training, the exercises are progressive, and build upon each other. That is, the output of the exercise for Unit 1 will be the input for the exercise in Unit 2. If you're developing training for a toolkit instead of an end-user application, you might make each exercise stand on its own. Since end-user training is more common, we'll proceed from that assumption.

Save a version of the data after each exercise while writing the exercises. For example, suppose your database is called `customer.db`. After you develop Exercise 1, you would:

1. Save `customer.db`

2. Make a copy of `customer.db` and name it as `customer1.db`

3. Reopen `customer.db` and continue developing the exercises with `customer.db`

Extended Example of Exercise Directions

The following example is the second part of a three-part exercise. The exercise was broken into parts so that each part used only one screen. This part uses the 'Bond Window'. Notice that the directions begin by reminding you what you did in the previous exercise. Also, they end by telling you what is next. This helps to place the exercise in the workflow.

The first line in each step contains the action to be performed. Results and comments appear on the second line, as in Step 8.

When multiple fields need to be filled in, those fields are listed in a simple table along with the values to be entered. The fields are listed in the order the reader will encounter them. Step 9 provides a good example.

"Exercise 4, Part 2: Create a Bond Trade

In the previous part of this exercise, you created a bond definition. In this part, you enter a bond trade based upon the definition that you created in Part 1.

This exercise gives detailed instructions for creating a trade. In future exercises, the directions for creating bond trades will be abbreviated. You may want to refer to these directions during those later exercises.

First, you will create the bond trade. Then, you will review the information that is automatically generated from the trade.

1. From the main menu, select **Trades | Create Trade**.
2. Select the **Bonds** tab.
3. Select the **Trades** button. This brings up the **Securities** window.
4. Select the **Find** button.
5. For the filter, select **US_BOND**.
6. Select the **Search** button.
7. From the search results, highlight your bond.
8. Select the **Open** button.
   The **Bond Trade** window can also be accessed by selecting | **Trades | Derivatives | Bond**.

9. Enter the following information in the **Market** tab:

Field	Enter this Data
Market Type:	Secondary
Book:	MYBOND1
Counterparty:	TRADEPARTNER

10. Enter the following information in the **Details** tab. Press [*Tab*] and the yield is calculated:

Field	Enter this Data
Purchase/Sell:	Purchase
Quantity:	1,000,000
Price:	100-00

11. From the **File** menu, select **Save**.

Saving the bond generates a transaction ID, which is displayed in the upper left corner of the window.

The Bond window is partially populated with information generated from the corresponding Bond Template. In the next section, you will review this information.

(Continued...)"

Writing Style for Directions

Directions for the in-class exercises need to be written in a style that is clear, simple, and consistent. In the following subsections, we'll talk about writing directions in a clear, concise style.

Sentence Structure: Put Conditional Phrases First

A conditional phrase makes a sentence depend upon a condition. For example, consider the sentence "If you know the customer's last name, enter the first part or the customer's entire last name"; the conditional phrase is "If you know the customer's last name".

If a sentence has a conditional phrase, put it first. This ensures that the reader knows what condition must be met before trying to perform the instruction. In the following sentence, the conditional phrase is underlined. Imagine that someone is reading you these directions as you perform the task, and I think you'll agree that the writer should have put the conditional phrase first:

> Cut the red wire leading to the detonator, <u>after making sure the blue wire is disconnected</u>.

In most software courses, the consequences of not putting the conditional phrase first are not so great. However, it is still a good practice.

Start Each Numbered Step with an Action

Begin each step with an action, like this:

> 1. Press [*F2*] or select **File | New | Claim**.

Putting the action up front, right after the number, ensures that the reader does not need to search the rest of the paragraph for the action to perform.

State the Result of Each Action

End each step with a result, like this:

> 1. Press [*F2*] or select **File | New | Claim**.
>
>   When the **New Claim** window opens, the cursor should be in the first field, **Last Name**.

Stating what the reader should see after performing an action is very reassuring. These results are signposts that tell the readers that they are on the right path.

If you separate the action and result with some white space, as in the example, the readers can easily make out when they reach the end of an action.

Use the Second Person

When writing in the second person, you write as if you are speaking directly to the person right now. For example, this book is written in the second person. Note that when writing in the second person, you use the word 'you' a lot. That's fine, because no word gets the reader's attention as surely as 'you'.

Some people consider second person too informal for a business document. Instead of "You should not hand off the claim without determining the type they prefer", "One should not hand off..." or "The claim should not be handed off..." is used. Writing in the third person like this is more formal, but also less effective.

No matter how you write the instructions, your reader will translate them into the second person. So if you write "One should not hand off... ", your reader will translate the passage in his or her mind into "You should not hand off... ". Save your reader the translation and just write in the second person.

Also, writing in the third person, such as "The claim should be handed off... " does not tell you who performs the action. Who hands off the claim? This is called the passive voice. It's a way to avoid stating who must perform an action. However, by not stating who must perform each action in your instructions, you leave the reader with unanswered questions. Make sure every instruction indicates who performs the action.

Differentiate Button Pushes, Menu Items, and the Text Displayed on Screen

In our example, button pushes are indicated by italics in square brackets: [*F2*]. Menu items and text that appears on screen are indicated by a bold font, like this: **File | New | Claim**. Use a distinctive font for screen text because the reader is going to be looking for that text on screen, and then comparing it to what you have written. The distinctive font makes it easy to find on the page, when your reader is looking back and forth between the screen and page.

Separate Nested Menu Items

Notice that nested menu items are separated by a '|' (pipe) sign. This is fine for most user courses. However, the pipe character has a special meaning in UNIX, so avoid doing this if the clients are working on a UNIX platform (that includes Linux). You can use the '>' (greater-than) sign instead.

Action

It's time to write the first draft of the exercises. Open the exercise descriptions in your word processor, launch the training application, and start stepping through the exercises.

Write the instructions as you perform them. Save a snapshot of the training files after each exercise.

Test and Revise the Exercise Files

When you finish writing the first draft of the exercises, your data and application file will be in the same condition as a student who has just finished the class. Take a final snapshot of the data and get ready to step through the exercises again.

Return the Training Files and Development Workstation to its Pre-Class Condition

For this test, you must start with a 'clean' system. Your starting point should be the same as that of your students'. You will need to return the training software environment to the condition it was in before you started writing the exercises. This includes not only the training application and data files, but also any supporting applications and files. For example, if you use a text editor or spreadsheet in the class, you must return them to their starting configurations.

Step Through the Exercise Directions

From start to finish, step through the exercises exactly as the students will be doing in the class. The goal is to re-create the same experience that the students will have. Consider doing this test with one of the subject matter experts who approved the exercise narrative. This will help to ensure that the exercises are correct, and that the goals for the exercises have been met.

During this test, you should need to make only minor corrections to the exercises. Major changes to the exercises will require you to rewrite and get buy-in on a new scenario.

Checkpoint

At this point, you have developed:

- An audience analysis that tells you who needs to be trained

- The learning objectives, which consist mostly of tasks the students must learn

- One or more measurable criteria for success for each learning objective

- A business scenario that will give your clients a realistic experience in the classroom

- A short description of an exercise for each learning objective that will teach that objective

- The application's starting point for the class

- Step-by-step directions for each in-class exercise

Action

Test and revise the exercise directions using the method given above. Start with a clean system, step through the exercises, and rewrite any directions that are incorrect or unclear.

Summary

In this chapter we looked at how to craft exercises that will be valuable learning exercises for our students. We learned the importance of preparing students' computers so they are ready for the exercises.

We then looked at write up instructions for exercises. Finally, we saw the importance of testing exercises and revising them.

The most important part is done! After this chapter, you have completed the heart of the course. The lectures and demonstrations that you develop later will support these exercises. You're well on the way to the finished course.

4

Develop Lectures

At this point, you are ready to start writing the lecture and demonstration that precedes each exercise. We assume that you will deliver the lecture and demo with the aid of an overhead projector, and that you will use some type of electronic slide show.

The temptation is to start at the beginning and develop an introductory lecture for the course. However, we are going to take a lot more structured, formulaic approach for developing the lectures.

Develop Lectures Around the Exercises

Remember that the exercises are central to the course. Each exercise teaches a procedure, or task. So we'll start with the first exercise, and develop the lecture to complement that exercise. After the lecture, we'll develop a demo. For each chapter or unit, you will first deliver the lecture and then the demonstration in the class. Your students will then complete the exercise.

A Structured Approach to Developing Lectures

For each unit develop an electronic slide show to support your lecture. You can use whatever slide-show software works best for you.

For this example, we will start with the first unit in our course, "Creating a New Customer". We have already developed an exercise for this task.

Launch your slide-show software and create a new slide show. Using the list below as a guide, create new slides.

> This list is just a guide. If any slide's topic is inappropriate for your subject, you can delete it. If you need several slides to cover the same topic, then do add them.

List of Suggested Slides

The following list gives you the title of each slide followed by a brief description of the information that should appear on the slide. Use this as a guide for creating your slide.

Unit Title

This is the title slide for the unit. Name the unit after the business task being taught. For example, "*Creating New Customers*" or "*Entering Initial Claim Information*".

If the title is not self-explanatory, you can add one or two lines of description.

Purpose

State the business purpose of the procedure. This may be obvious from the title of the unit, but you should still include it for every unit to be consistent. To avoid repeating the unit title, try to state the purpose of the unit without using any of the terms from the title slide. In our example, you might say something like the following:

> "To accurately enter a new customer's information into the system, and save that information for later use."

Or:

> "To accurately enter all information needed to begin the processing of a new claim."

When is This Procedure Performed?

State the conditions or situation that triggers this procedure. For example, "You enter new customer information upon receiving a completed and approved Form NC1 from Sales" or "You enter new claim information upon being connected to a claimant by the New Claims department".

Who Performs this Procedure?

Your class may comprise people with differing job functions. Unless you know that everyone in the class has identical duties, you should include this slide. For example, you might state, "New customer information is entered only by Level 1 Customer Service Representatives".

What Information is Entered During this Procedure?

During every procedure, the users must enter some information. Even if the users are only looking up information, they must still enter a search condition. List the information that the users must enter during this procedure. The users can check this list before starting the procedure to ensure that all the information needed to complete the procedure successfully is available.

What Processing does the System Perform on the Data Entered During this Procedure?

What happens to the data that the users enter? Is it just saved to a database? Is it used to calculate other values? Does it populate specific reports? When users understand how the data they enter is used by the system, they become more confident with the system. They are also better able to recognize the results of bad data, and to troubleshoot problems. In our example, you might state how the customer information is used later in the system: to contact the customer, bill the customer, determine payouts in case of an accident, and so on.

What is the Result of this Procedure?

State the end result of this procedure. Phrase the result in business terms, not technical terms. For example, instead of writing "A new record is added to the database", write, "A new customer is added to the system".

Special Fields

Identify any special fields in the data entry screen(s) for this procedure. Special fields include:

- *Required fields*: The process cannot be completed without entering data into these fields.

- *Not-obvious fields*: Any field whose purpose is not obvious from the field's name or position on screen. For example, does the field labeled **Type** refer to the customer type or type of insurance purchased?

- *Non-standard fields*: Any field that functions in a non-standard way. If the field behaves in a way that is different from the standards for user interfaces on the platform you are using, state how it functions.

Demonstration

This slide introduces the demonstration that you will perform. You may want to add a short description like this to this slide:

> "Demonstration: Entering the initial claim for an auto accident involving two drivers"

After showing this slide, perform the demo. Then, return to the slide show again.

Exercise

This slide introduces the exercise that the students perform in the class. You may want to include the following:

- The name of the exercise

- The page number in the Student Workbook

- The estimated time to complete the exercise

After showing this slide, assign the in-class exercise to the students. When they've finished the exercise, return to the slide show.

Review

This slide reminds the students what they learned in this unit. After the students complete the exercise, this slide brings them back to the discussion. Do not try to restate all of the information you delivered on this one slide. It is a reminder, not a restatement.

Questions?

This slide is just a reminder to pause and ask the class if they have any questions before moving on to the next unit.

Checkpoint

At this point, you have developed:

- An audience analysis that tells you who needs to be trained
- The learning objectives, which consist mostly of tasks the students must learn
- One or more measurable criteria for success for each learning objective
- A business scenario that will give your clients a realistic experience in the classroom
- A short description of an exercise for each learning objective that will teach that objective
- The application's starting point for the class
- For each in-class exercise, step-by-step directions

Action

For each unit in the course, develop a slide show. Use the list of slides above as a guideline.

Summary

In this chapter we developed lectures to introduce each exercise. We learned to use a standard lecture plan to give each lecture a proven structure that can be applied quickly to any exercise.

The lecture leaves space for a demonstration to take place part way through. Let's now turn our attention to developing the demo in the next chapter.

5

Develop the Demo

In a software class, usually the best way to teach how to perform a task is by demonstrations. This section discusses how to develop an effective teaching demonstration.

Write the Demo Instructions

Remember that the purpose of the demo is to enable the students to complete the in-class exercise successfully. Therefore, your demo should *use the same core functions that the students will use during the exercise*.

Look through the exercise that you developed for this unit, and identify the menu options and functions that are essential for successfully completing the exercise. For example, if the purpose of the exercise is to create a new customer, the menu items that are used to create a new record and the required fields in the **New Customer** screen would be core functions. Any other optional information about the customer would not be a core function.

When writing your demo, you can literally make a copy of the directions for the exercise. Then change the data that is used while working with the core functions. In our example, you would change data like the customer's name, address, type of policy, etc.

The result of this process is a demo that should have:

- The same core functions as the exercise
- Different data from the exercise that does not interfere with or affect the data used in the exercise
- Some optional functions, which are not repeated in the exercise

Use Unique Data for the Demo

Some students will just watch during your demo. Others will duplicate your steps on their computer as you demonstrate. Therefore, the demo should leave the data that will be used in the upcoming exercises totally untouched. That is, data changed by the demo should not affect the data used in any of the exercises.

You may be tempted to accomplish this by using a different database or files for the demos and exercises. That would definitely segregate your demo and exercise data. However, it also requires the instructor to switch between two different databases/files. This may present a problem for the students who want to follow the demo on their own machines. Before embracing this approach, you must ensure that the students can easily switch databases/files.

Developing a Demo—Key Steps

When developing the demonstration that precedes an in-class exercise, follow this method:

1. Make a copy of the step-by-step directions for the exercise. Use this copy as the starting point for the demonstration.

2. Identify the core functionality that the student must know to complete the exercise successfully. What menu items and functions must the student learn?

3. Delete any optional functionality from the copy of the directions. Remove steps that use any menu items or functions that the student does not need to know.

4. Change the data in the copy, so that the demo uses different data from the exercise. Ensure that the demo data does not interfere with or affect the exercise data.

5. Consider adding optional functionality that you think will enhance the demo. Try to use different optional functionality than that used in the exercise.

Write the Demo Speaking Points

To ensure a smooth demo, the instructor must know more than what keys to press. The instructor must also know what to say. The instructor must narrate the demonstration. An experienced instructor may be able to come up with a good narrative as he or she delivers the demo. Unless you know the instructor is capable of this, you should write speaking points for the instructor to use while delivering the demo.

These speaking points do not need to be a word-for-word script. However, they do need to include every piece of information, every fact, and concept that the instructor must convey during the demo.

For example, suppose the instructor is demonstrating creating a new claim. The process begins with selecting the menu item, **File | New Claim**. Your speaking points do not need to include the fact that the instructor is selecting **File | New Claim**, because the students can see that. However, you may want to include a speaking point about the fact that this menu item is available only to certain users at certain times.

How to Write Demo Speaking Points

In your word processor, create a two-column table. Label the right column `Steps`, `Activity`, or something similar. Label the left column `Speaking Points`, `Discussion points`, or something similar.

In each cell of the right column, place a step or group of steps from the demo. In each cell of the left column, place the speaking point(s) for that step(s).

You will include this document in the Instructor Guide.

Example of Demo Directions with Speaking Points

The following table is an example of demo directions and speaking points. Notice that the `Discussion Point` column contains a word-by-word script for the instructor. Depending upon how expert your instructor is with the material, and upon how consistent you want the course to be from one session to another, you can write the discussion points in several ways:

- *Word-by-word scrip*
  Most appropriate for inexperienced instructors and most consistent from session to session.

- *Detailed notes*
  Contains every fact that should be covered, but not in script format. Appropriate for any instructor, where you want to ensure that a list of concepts and facts is communicated to the students.

- *Brief notes*
  Contain reminders to cover areas of material and concepts. Ideal for an experienced instructor who can customize delivery on the fly to the unique needs of each group of students.

Step	Discussion Point	Instructor Activity
1.	Say you want to find all companies whose name begins with **Acme**. The function-key method won't work for finding multiple companies, because it forces you to select a single company. So, we use the wildcard, the asterisk (*).	Click the **Company Name** field.
2.	Notice that you can click only in the shaded line.	1. With the insertion point in the **Company Name** field, type **Acme***.
		2. Press [*Enter*]. All companies whose names begin with **Acme** are displayed.

Step	Discussion Point	Instructor Activity
3.	Let's conduct a more specific search. We'll search for any company whose **Legal Status** field is not empty. We would do this because in our system, any company whose legal status is not okay has an entry in this field. A non-entry in this field indicates the company is okay. We'll clear the previous search by pressing [*F7*].	
4.	Pose the question: If we were unsure what the **Legal Status** or some other field told us about the client, where would we look to get this information?	1. Press [*F7*]. 2. Click on the **Page 1** tab. 3. In the **Legal Status** field, type *. 4. Press [*Enter*]. All companies that have an entry in the **Legal Status** field are called up. 5. Clear the search by pressing [*F7*].

Checkpoint

At this point, you have developed:

- An audience analysis that tells you who needs to be trained

- The learning objectives, which consist mostly of tasks the students must master

- One or more measurable criteria for success for each learning objective

- A business scenario that will give your clients a realistic experience in the classroom

- A short description of an exercise for each learning objective that will teach that objective; one exercise may be used to teach a number of closely-related objectives

- For each exercise, an electronic slide show that includes many or all of the suggested slides; each slide show/exercise combination is now called a unit or chapter

- For each unit, a detailed in-class exercise that gives the students practice with the task(s) being learned in that unit

Action

Write the demo, as described above. The result should be a two-column document for each unit, with step-by-step directions in one column and speaking notes in the other.

Summary

In this chapter we saw how to prepare for live demonstrations in front of an audience. Key points included writing a demo that uses the same core functions as the student will use in the exercises and writing instructors' notes for performing demos.

In the next chapter we will start to tie all this preparation together into a set of comprehensive notes for both, the students and the instructors.

6

Package the Course

You need to create two packages for the course: a Student Guide and an Instructor Guide. The Student Guide is the simplest to create, so let's start there.

The Student Guide

The Student Guide consists of five parts:

- The table of contents
- An introduction
- Printouts of the slides used in the class
- Directions for the in-class exercises
- A listing of resources and contacts for getting help after the class

The following subsections describe each part in detail.

Table of Contents

Generate the table of contents after you have assembled the other parts of the Student Guide. If your word processing software gives you the option, also generate a table of graphics when you generate the table of contents. This will make it easier for students to find screenshots when they use the Student Guide for reference.

Introduction

The introduction will help students ensure that they are the right people to attend the class, that they are prepared for it, and that it will be relevant to them.

State the Goals of the Course

At the beginning of the course development process, you established an overall goal for the course. You also established learning objectives for each unit of the course. In the introduction, include a section that states these goals. Consider using a table that lists each unit in the left column and the goals for each unit in the right column.

Describe the Intended Audience

Who should attend your course? Is it for people with specific job titles? Is the course only for employees, or can contractors and vendors also attend? Are there parts of the course that would be appropriate for the managers or for those who work upstream or downstream of the students? This section of the introduction should answer those questions.

List Prerequisites

The introduction should list any prerequisite knowledge and skills the student must have before taking the course. This may include:

- Proficiency with the operating environment
- Proficiency with third-party applications used in the class
- An understanding of business processes specific to the student's workplace

For example, the students in our fictional course might need to be able to the following:

- Navigate folders and directories in their PCs and on the network
- Use a spreadsheet application to set up basic formulas
- Understand their company's business processes for processing claims

Each prerequisite should be specific enough so that it could be tested, if needed. For example, the prerequisite "*Use basic file management functions*" cannot be tested; it is too vague. However, the prerequisite "From within the **File | Open** dialog box, navigate to a network folder and open a file" is specific enough to be tested.

Knowledge and skills are not the only types of prerequisites that you must include. Include any software or hardware that the students must have access. For example, the students might need user IDs and passwords for the application, or they might need to bring their own laptops to the class. List these prerequisites as well.

Duration and Class Size

State the expected duration of the class and the number of students for which it is designed. The information helps your students to fit the class into their schedules.

Training Group Contact Information

The introduction should include contact information for the persons responsible for the course. This includes the:

- Course author (you)

- Instructors (possibly also you)

- Person(s) to contact to enroll in the course (maybe also you)

- Authority figures who sponsored the course (if it's an internal course)

Printouts of the Slides

The student guide should contain printouts of the slides used in the class. Each unit, or chapter, will have its own slide show.

> Your presentation application may be able to print handouts, with several slides per page and space reserved for taking notes. Check the application's online help under **handouts**, and **printing**.

Directions for the In-class Exercises

Each unit, or chapter, will probably have its own student exercise. Each exercise follows a slide show. Print out each exercise and place it after the appropriate slide show.

Resources and Contacts

The goal of every software class is to enable the students to become independently productive. A list of resources where students can get help with the software supports this goal. The list can include links to online help, where to obtain documentation for the software, and contact information for people who can assist the students.

The Instructor Guide

The Instructor Guide consists of the same five parts as the Student Guide. However, the Instructor Guide has additional information to each of the parts.

When developing the Instructor Guide, start with a copy of the Student Guide and add the information below.

Table of Contents

In addition to a table of contents, generate a table of the units and their learning objectives. The instructor should be able to look in the beginning of the Guide and see all of the learning objectives.

Most word processors use paragraph styles to generate a table of contents. In a similar way, you can use paragraph styles to generate a table of learning objectives. Check the online help for your word processor under **indexes and tables**.

Introduction

The introduction contains all of the information that a student needs to decide whether to attend the course. You can copy and paste this information into your public announcement of the class.

Also, include login information for any accounts used in class. This includes the accounts for the instructor and the students, and any administrative accounts needed to set up the system.

Printouts of the Slides

For the Student Guide, you printed the slide show for each unit. You may have used your presentation application to print handouts with several slides per page and space reserved for taking notes.

Most presentation applications also enable you to include speaking notes for each slide. These notes are for the instructor only. They are printed when you select the Notes view of the slide show. Print the slides and speaking notes for the Instructor Guide. The students get printouts of the slides with space for taking notes, and the instructor gets a printout with speaking notes.

Directions for the In-class Exercises

In the Student Guide, you included directions for each in-class exercise after each slide show. When teaching each unit, the instructor will show the slides, then work through the demonstration, and then assign the in-class exercise.

For each unit, place the directions for the demonstration between the slide show and the exercise. This is the order in which each unit will be delivered: slide show, demo, student practice exercise.

Resources and Contacts

There is nothing you need to add to this section for the Instructor Guide. However, you may want to demonstrate some of the online resources available to the students.

Slide Show Files

What application did you use to create the slide show? Are you sure that the application is installed on the instructor's computer? If so, you can just copy the files to the instructor's computer.

If you're not sure that the instructor's computer will have the slide show software, export the slide show in a format that will work on any computer. For example, Microsoft PowerPoint has a Pack and Go function that will package the slide show player with a slide show. OpenOffice can export a slide show in a format that plays in a Web browser. Your slide show application may have a similar function.

Checkpoint

At this point, you have developed:

- An audience analysis to tells you who needs to be trained

- The learning objectives, which consist mostly of tasks the students must master

- One or more measurable criteria for success for each learning objective

- A business scenario that will give your clients a realistic experience in the classroom

- A short description of an exercise for each learning objective that will teach that objective; one exercise may be used to teach several closely related objectives

- An electronic slide show for each exercise that includes many or all of the suggested slides; each slide show/exercise combination is now called a unit or chapter

- A detailed in-class exercise for each unit, that gives the students practice with one or more tasks being learned in that unit

- A demo for each unit with detailed directions for the instructor

- Speaking points for each demo

Action

Write and package the Student Guide, as described above. Students will use this document in the class, and take it with them after class.

Then, make a copy of the Student Guide and save it as the Instructor Guide. Make the changes and additions described above.

If needed, package the slide show in a format that will play on the instructor's computer.

Summary

In this chapter, we saw how to create guides for students and instructors, giving your course a lasting value for students—and freeing you from being the only person who can deliver it.

We saw the main things to include in the Student Guide and then supplemented that with additional material to form the Instructor Guide.

Your preparation is almost complete. We now prepare to deliver the course.

7

Setup and Test Run

Every course writer and instructor would like to have a complete, start-to-finish test run of every course they deliver. Unfortunately, today's tight budgets and aggressive timelines don't always allow for a thorough test run of every course. The development method that you have followed minimizes the chance of surprises when the course is delivered. However, you should still try to perform all or at least some of the pre-class tasks below.

Test the Room Setup

You don't know for sure if the course software will run on the instructor and student computers until you have tested it. For example, consider teaching a web-based application. In this case, the firewall or security settings in the browser might prevent the application from functioning properly. If the software must be installed on the training room computers, you may need to deal with issues like disk space, memory, and missing .dll files.

You should also test the projector for the training room. Some software is designed to be run at high resolution, such as 1024 by 768 pixels. Test the projector to ensure it has enough resolution to display the application and slide show.

Practice Run

The best kind of practice run is giving the course to a portion of your audience. If you have the opportunity to give the course to a small audience, then do this.

If you cannot test the course on a subset of your audience, consider delivering the course to an empty room. That may sound strange, but this method works. Hearing yourself deliver the lectures and demos aloud is an effective way to test the material you've written. Time yourself. It's an effective way to determine how long each lecture/demo will take.

Step through the student exercises. Do them in the same order the students will. Does the data from one exercise flow into the next? Are the functions used in each exercise covered in the lecture/demo? How long does each exercise take? After the practice run, you might want to revise your estimate of the course duration.

Finally, reset the computer(s) that you used during your practice run. Return them to the condition they should be in at the beginning of the class. This is a good test of your refresh routine.

Action

Test the room setup as described above. Deliver the course to a small test group or an empty room. Step through the exercises yourself when you do this. Pay special attention to the flow of data from one exercise to another and to the applicability of the lecture/demos to the exercises.

Develop Follow-up Materials

Earlier, you developed criteria that will be used to determine the course's success. For example, you may have determined that the students need to do the following:

- Pass a written test
- Perform the process taught in front of an instructor
- Perform the process taught while on the job

At this point, you should develop the tools needed to measure these criteria. That is, you should:

- Write the test that the students must pass
- Develop the task they must perform in front of the instructor at the end of the class

- Write the form the students' supervisors will use to evaluate the students' on-the-job proficiency

You should get buy-in from the course sponsors on whatever test or form you develop. It is the sponsors who agreed to the course's criteria for success. They should also understand and agree to the methods used to measure those criteria.

Example of a Follow-up Course Evaluation

Most course evaluations measure only the students' satisfaction with the course. The evaluation asks the students to rate things such as the length, clarity, and focus of the course. This kind of evaluation is useful to the course developer, because it enables the developer to improve student satisfaction with the course. However, it is not of much use to the upper-level sponsors of the course.

The sponsors of your course are more interested in whether the course supported your company's business objectives. Did it increase productivity? Did it decrease errors? Did it enable people to perform analysis that they could not perform before? When you know what business objectives you are measuring, the questions suggest themselves.

Entire books are devoted to measuring a course's effectiveness and return on investment. A complete treatment is beyond the scope of this document. If you want to know more, look for training books that focus on evaluation, assessment, and return on investment.

The first five questions of the example below measure student satisfaction with a training course. Questions six through ten measure how well the course supported the company's business objectives. This evaluation is designed to be filled out after the students have returned to their workplace and put their training to use. Feel free to use this example as a starting point for your own course evaluations:

"This course evaluation will take only a few minutes of your time. We would like you to rate the quality and usefulness of the course you attended. There are no right or wrong answers. Your response will be used to improve future courses. Thank you for participating!

1. *Were the goals for this course, as stated in the course announcement, met?*

    a. No. The goals stated in the course announcement were not met.

    b. Yes. The goals stated in the course announcement were met.

    c. I cannot say, because I did not read the course announcement or had no idea what the goals of this course were.

2. *The amount of material covered in this course was:*

    a. Too little. I would have like to know more about the module being taught.

    b. Just right. There was enough material to enable me to use the module effectively, without overwhelming me.

    c. Too much. I was overwhelmed by the amount of material.

3. *The pace of the course was:*

    a. Too slow.

    b. Just right.

    c. Too fast.

4. *Was the presentation given by the instructor clear to you?*

    a. Somewhat. I understood some of the instructions, but most of what was taught I did not understand.

    b. Mostly. I understood most of what was taught, but some of the material we covered was still unclear to me when I left the class.

    c. Completely. All of the material that was covered in the class was clear to me when I left.

5. Did the class offer you enough opportunity to practice what you learned in the class?

    a. No. I would have liked more opportunity to practice in the class.

    b. Yes. The class offered enough opportunity to practice the material covered.

6. Did you increase your usage of our online system as a result of attending this class?

    a. No. Since attending this class, I use the online system no more than before, or intend to use it no more than before.

    b. Yes. Because of what I learned in the class, I use or plan to use the online system more often than before.

    c. This question doesn't apply to me.

7. As a result of this class, are you able to spend less time performing the task covered? For example, are you able to spend less time creating a purchase order or travel request, or less time looking for ledgers to view?

    a. No. It takes me just as long to perform the same tasks as before taking this class.

    b. Yes. I can perform the tasks covered in the class in less time than before.

    c. This question doesn't apply to me.

8. Has your usage of the online system increased your accuracy when performing the task covered? For example, is the information you submit on purchase requests or travel requests more accurate? Are you able to get more accurate information from online ledgers?

    a. The information I submit for transactions, or get from the system, is less accurate than when I was using a paper-based form.

    b. The information that I enter or receive from the system is more accurate than when I was using a paper-based system.

    c. The accuracy of the information that I enter or receive from the system is about the same as when I was using a paper-based system.

9. *Since class, have you been able to teach your coworkers how to use the online system, or to help them use the system?*

    a. No. I have not been able to teach or help my coworkers when they needed it.

    b. Yes. Using what I learned in the class, I have been able to teach or help my coworkers to use the system.

    c. This question doesn't apply to me, because I have not needed to teach or help anyone else with the system.

10. *Were your questions about finance, travel, or other kinds of policy adequately answered in the class?*

    a. No. I left the class with unanswered questions about policy, and they were not followed up on.

    b. Yes. My questions about policy were answered in class or by a follow-up after class.

    c. I did not have any policy questions."

Checkpoint

At this point, you have:

- Developed an audience analysis that tells you who needs to be trained
- Written the learning objectives, which consist mostly of tasks the students must master
- Developed one or more measurable criteria for success for each learning objective
- Developed a business scenario that will give your clients a realistic experience in the classroom

- Written an exercise for each learning objective that will teach that objective; one exercise may be used to teach several closely related objectives

- Written an electronic slide show for each exercise, which includes many or all of the suggested slides; each slide show/exercise combination is now called a unit or chapter

- Developed a demo with detailed directions and speaking points for the instructor for each unit

- Written and packaged Student Guide

- Written and packaged Instructor Guide

- Packaged slide-show in a format that will play on the instructor's computer

- Tested room setup

- Delivered the course to a small test group, or even an empty room; while doing so, you have stepped through the exercises yourself

Action

Edit the course material based on feedback from your practice run.

Develop the tools needed to measure the criteria for success. Get the sponsors' buy-in on the methods used to measure success of the course.

Summary

We are now almost ready to give the course. In this chapter we saw how to prepare for the course's delivery. Key points included ensuring that the room and equipment are ready and practicing the whole presentation, preferably in front of an audience and wherever possible in the room where the course will be delivered.

Developing follow-up materials that will help you to measure your course's effectiveness and to establish that your students can now perform the required tasks is another key point.

If you have been through all the preparation stages so far, you will be in an excellent position to deliver your course. Let's turn our attention to that now.

8

Deliver the Course

Throughout this book, we looked at the essential qualities of successful training courses. We looked at a systematic process for creating successful training courses and covered the first six of the seven steps from setup to delivery. We now reach the last stage of the process namely, delivering the course.

Presenting your Course

A complete course in public speaking is beyond the scope of this document. However, there are a few important points to remember when presenting a software class.

> There are many excellent web articles that deal with general presentation skills. For some clear, punchy articles on the subject try the Marketing Professionals web site (www.marketingprofs.com).

First, keep the tone of the class consultative. Instead of assuming the attitude of "I am the instructor and I am teaching these students this material", assume the attitude of "I am a consultant who is teaching my clients to solve this business problem". You're not teaching a class; you're leading a work session. This consultative attitude is very effective at winning over your students. It conveys a sense of professionalism and caring about their needs.

Second, don't be afraid to answer a question with, "I don't know. I'll research the answer and get back to you." If possible, find out the answers to questions you don't know during the next break in the class, and tell the students in the class. If you can't do that, research the question immediately after class and follow up. Collect the e-mail addresses of everyone in your classes, and send them all the answers to any questions that you could not answer in the class. This kind of follow-up builds credibility even better than knowing all the answers in class. No one will be surprised to discover that there are limits to your knowledge. But almost everyone will be pleasantly surprised by a prompt, thorough follow-up to his or her unanswered questions.

Third, avoid unexplored territory in the software. Sometimes we are so eager to please a class that we take on a question that we have not prepared for. We look for the answer to a question under menus that we have not studied, or by trying program functions that we have not rehearsed. Do this kind of exploring during a break or after class. During class, stay on the path that you have planned. Don't risk damaging your credibility by floundering in unexplored areas of the application.

Fourth, don't allow students who insist upon following your demonstrations on their computers to slow the rest of the class. Many times, students want to duplicate the steps that you are demonstrating on their computers. That is fine, except when they continually interrupt to ask you to repeat the last step.

The problem is that while you are demonstrating step two, instead of watching you, these students are performing step one on their own computers. They miss the instructions that you are giving because they are too busy duplicating the instructions that you just gave. As a result, they repeatedly ask you to repeat the last step that you demonstrated.

You should encourage these students to stop duplicating your demo on their computers, and instead to watch closely and take notes. Reassure them that they will have a chance to practice during the in-class exercises.

Summary

One of the keys to being a confident presenter is to remain within your capabilities and stay in control. The tips we've seen here, as well as some background reading on presentation skills, will help you achieve this.

9
A Final Note

When you are developing and preparing to deliver a software class, it's tempting to focus only on how to use the software. Remember that software doesn't get used in a vacuum. It gets used in business situations to solve real business problems. Learning about your students' situation and how they can use the software to address their business needs is the difference between a good class and a great class. This extra effort also makes the difference between just conveying information to your students, and really connecting with them. And at the end of a hard day in the classroom, you can ask for nothing better than to have connected with your students, and made their lives easier and more productive.

Index

less general than the IT books you have seen in the past. Our unique business model allows us to bring you more focused information, giving you more of what you need to know, and less of what you don't.

Packt is a modern, yet unique publishing company, which focuses on producing quality, cutting-edge books for communities of developers, administrators, and newbies alike. For more information, please visit our website: www.PacktPub.com.